How To Be A Geek

Murphy
Diddle

This book is dedicated to my fellow friends- from Tate's to Webb. - JMD

How To Be A Geek

Murphy Diddle

Introduction

Hi! I'm Murphy! This book will teach you how to be a geek in just 4 steps! Also, there will be some fun games you can play with your friends. I hope you enjoy this book.

Sincerely,
Murphy Diddle, Author

Step One: Know your Basic Video Games

The first thing you need to know is your basic video games. Games such as Pong, Pac-Man and Minecraft are classified as basic games, due to their popularity. Game series such as Sonic, Mario and Zelda are basic game series, also due to their popularity. If you've never played video games before, search up the game titles and series I addressed on YouTube for videos.

Step Two: Know Your Consoles

Good! You know your basic games! Now get ready to learn about the consoles!

Now, the basic consoles of today are the Xbox One, PS4 a.k.a. Playstation 4, and the new Nintendo Switch. The game I addressed earlier called Minecraft is on all three of those consoles. But some consoles have specific titles. For example, the Nintendo Switch has Splatoon 2, and no other console has Splatoon 2. And for the Xbox One, it has Kinect Sports Rivals. But the PS4 has Ace Combat 7. Games like these are only for those consoles, and those consoles only.

Step Three: Get Twitch

What is Twitch? Twitch is a game streaming app for

iOS, Android, Xbox 360, Xbox One, PS3 and PS4. Twitch is where you can watch people play your favorite games live.

Step Four: Make A YouTube Channel

Now, this will be a little bit tricky. 1. Go to YouTube.com. 2. Click Sign In. If you have a Google Account, sign in and skip to step 5. 3. Now, choose the option to create a Google account.

4.Follow the steps to create a Google account. 5. In the top right corner of the screen, click on your profile icon and then the 'Settings' cog icon. 6.Under your settings, you'll see the option "Create a channel," and click on the "Create a channel" link.

Now you can choose to make a personal channel, buisness channel or a channel with another name. 7. Now, name your channel and select a category.(P.S. This will also create a Google+ account.) Ta-da! You've created a YouTube account. 8. Get some channel art. Your banner art should be about 2560x1440, and your channel profile art should be 800x800.

Super Hard Questions To Challenge Your Geek Friends

Question 1: What years were all Fallout games released?

Answer: 1997, 1998, 2008, 2010, 2015.

Question 2: What month and year was the first video game invented?

Answer: October 1958

Notes:

www.ingramcontent.com/pod-product-compliance
Lightning Source LLC
Chambersburg PA
CBHW041635050326
40689CB00024B/4975